MW00424509

THE FIGHTER

Helle Gade

BUTTERDRAGONS
PUBLISHING

Title: The Fighter
Author: Helle Gade

Published by Butterdragons® Publishing
https://butterdragons.com

ISBN: 9789493229549 (ebook)
ISBN: 9789493229556 (hardback)
ISBN: 9789493229563 (audio book)

Cover Design by: Dazed Designs

Audio book narrated by Martha Webb

Dedication

To Ira Myriam. Love you girl!

For Helle, with love

There was a girl and she had glorious dreams. But dark clouds descended upon the girl and shattered her dreams. She wandered aimlessly imprisoned by her curse. She lost herself. She wandered and wandered, her prison becoming smaller and smaller. What would she do?

As she wandered, she stubbed her toe on something and screamed. What was that? She leaned down and felt for the offensive object. It was a book. She felt something stirring inside of her chest. Her heart fluttered. Maybe not all was lost of her?

As she opened the book, the words started flowing and the images jumping at her. She giggled and startled herself. Could it be? Could it be that her dreams are still alive and achievable? It certainly seemed so.

So, she sat down and started reading. Reading and reading. And she didn't want to stop. So, she read some more. And she read until there were no more pages and words left. But she desired more. What was she to do? Suddenly, a pen and paper appeared in her hands. She laid the paper on the ground and tried to write but no words came out. She became sad and tears gathered in her eyes.

But then, she heard a tiny voice in the back of her mind, "Don't be afraid. You can do this. Just write. Express your feelings and your thoughts. Have no fear, you will be glorious."

Slowly, she took the pen and pressed the tip against the paper. And the magic happened! Her hand started moving and the words pouring out on the paper. And they were glorious. The girl transcended into her dreams and found herself.

Her words remained and each person who read her words was left in awe by her amazingness.

by BDP Authors

Pain

My Story

Spreading my wings

Releasing butterfly dust

Creating a colourful pattern

On the white paper

I'm telling my story

Bit by jagged bit

Pain and happiness

Mixing

Into a strange tale

Burning Needles

Pain bearing down on me
An army of burning needles
Searing their way into my skin
Into my muscles and bones

Breathing becomes hard rapidly
The shallow breaths leave me dizzy
As I pull myself into foetal position
Clutching my knees to my chest

As I slip into unconsciousness
I pray to wake up whole
Both in body and mind
A simple wish

Solitaire

Teardrops on a broken window
Bloody shards of glass
A scream in the night
Frustration in the air
Hands torn by anger
Pools of blood reflecting
A hunter with no prey
Standing solitaire
Without a beating heart

Cut

A tear along the seam

Stitches broken

Hearts ripped

By one word

A virulent feeling

Malignant intention

Said with insolent glee

Lunacy

Deliver me from this plane
This slaughterhouse of agony
Spreading like a vile malady

Unstoppable
All consuming

A curse I cannot escape
Since my heart has capitulated
And my mind has fled its confines

Unsavoury madness is inevitable
Invisible chains restricting

I'm delirious in my lunacy
Hallucinations of haunting misery
Swarm my mind like locusts

Deliver me from the suffering
Ease this vile malady
Take away the agony

Remembered Youth

There's no solace for me tonight
Old ghosts haunts me
Bringing back
What I'd rather forget

My stomach churns
When I think of the old days
My recklessness
A sore spot in my memories

We are all born
With the thought of immortality
There is nothing we cannot do
Or won't do

The elders try to give us wisdom
But we rarely listen
Because we are driven
By our unruly hormones

I despair over my actions

Wild and without thoughts of my future

I constantly wonder

What if I had been more careful?

But it is too late to change anything

My past is what it is

My future is a blank page

Perhaps redemption

Perhaps damnation

Monster

I don't want to hurt you
I have no choice
The darkness within me
Is more than I can contain

A writhing, living entity within me
Clawing at my humanity
Demanding to be let free
Taxing my reserves

Oh, sweet Gods have mercy
Let me control the monstrosity
That demands entrance to the world
Devouring all in in its path

Bullets

Bullet holes

Light shining through

A bloody world visible

Bodies scattered all over

Feeding the earth

With their cooling blood

The ultimate sacrifice

Unappreciated

Soon forgotten by the masses

The survivors

Left with the pain

With the memories

Of the brave souls

Laying down their lives

To protect others

Tears

I hide my tears
In the layers of the night
Slipping them in between
Midnight and dawn
Where all is silent
Only hushed sobs
Break the quietness
And sparkling tears
Light up the darkness
Resembling twinkling stars

Broken

I am broken

The pieces of me

Are ripped away

By the fierce

Northern wind

Scattered

To the four corners

Of the world

Impossible to retrieve

Once

What once was

Is now lost

I see the accusations

In the eyes of the dead

The haunting echo

Of precious life

Now tormenting

My crumbling mind

The silence is deafening

Eternal sleep evades me

In the darkness

I feel

Insignificant

Fear

Brain Fog

I walk around in a constant fog
My thoughts at the tip of my fingers
Yet, they feel farther away than the stars

Everything surrounding me is muted
Colourless and uninteresting
Like a distant dream you cannot recall

I feel neither sad nor happy
I'm merely existing in a haze
Walking where my feet pull me

It feels like I'm there for an eternity
Life flowing past me unnoticed
As if I have released the tethers to my body

Eventually, I will return
Desperately trying to catch up
Trying to integrate myself into the world again

Descend

Down, down, down
Ever so carefully
Putting one foot in front of the other
Full focus on the path ahead

Cannot look up
Must keep an eye on my feet
One rock can bring me down
And then I'm lost

My muscles are shaking
Sweat tickling down my back
Breathing hard
Under the merciless sun

Praying intensely to the Gods
Please let me make it down
Without getting sick
Without injury

Autopilot kicking in
Must not think of anything
Humming some tune
As I brave the terrible descend

The utter relief when I see the end
The utter horror as I see the final path
Must be so careful
Must not cry

Finally down
The relief is almost debilitating
As it courses through my body
Finally down

Drowning

I lie in shallow waters

Though it feels like

The weight of the ocean

Is keeping me down

I'm slowly drowning

Only reaching the surface

Once, every now and then

To take a cleansing breath of air

The Abyss

I walked among the pillars
In the darkest of nights
Towards the abyss

The time had come
To look into the darkness
That hid in the corners of my soul

The question was
Would I survive the journey
With my mind intact

Or would the horrors
Push my remaining sanity
Over the edge

Storm

The centre of the storm

Is a calm lake

In the mountains

Deceptively calm and cool

Promising rest and refreshment

Before the winds hit

Trying to tear you apart

With invisible hands

Forcing you to flee

To run from the carnage

Left in the wake of the storm

Vacuum

The cold beat against me relentlessly
Battering my poorly shielded soul
Time has seized to exist
Only an empty vacuum left behind

The stars have blinked for the last time
The sun now as cold as the moon
Just a gaping blackness
Threatening to swallow me whole

Life is as extinct as my hope
Loneliness and a desperate fear
That I'm destined to roam

In this endless black void
Forever alone

Lights On

Lying in the dark
With the overwhelming need
To turn on the light
But terrified of moving

Finally working up the courage
To reach out and flip the switch
Only to realize
That the light doesn't work

Knowing something is wrong
But still not able to figure it out

Finally understanding
That I'm still caught in the nightmare
Still sleeping

Making a conscious effort to wake up
To flip the switch and bathe in the light
Chasing away the horrid dream

Lost

I am lost

Ever so lost

A tree here

A tree there

No breadcrumbs

No yellow brick road

Lost

In a world

Where I am of no use

Damaged

Beyond repair

When?

Retracing my steps
Searching for the crucial point
Where it all changed forever

The point that altered my future
With drastic brush strokes
On the canvas, that is my life

How did it come to this?
Having to relearn how to live
Adapting to new circumstances

At the point in life
Where it should all be set
However
The fates had other ideas
When they made my life thread

No Shield

My skin feels paper-thin

Nothing shielding me

Against the world

Anymore

As if one comment

Could break me like a twig

I was once strong

A willow bending in the wind

I thought myself immortal

Living life to the fullest

It lasted for such a short time

I remember it with joy

But I also mourn it

As it is forever lost

Never to be found again

Stalked

Crushing blackness surrounding me
Not a whisper to be heard
Not a breeze to be felt

Alone in this desolate space
Confined in my twisted mind
A captive of my imagination

I cannot escape
It nips at my heels
Hunting me relentlessly

This darkness contains
All my fears
Ready to unleash them on me

Sable Silence

Thoughts leaking in the night
Burning their way
Through my broken shields

Tossing and turning
Trying to make sense of it all
Having to give up
At the first light of dawn

A new day full of insecurities
Tormenting me every moment
Through the daylight hours

Until the darkness comes
Until the silence is absolute
Until I'm alone again

Cosmic Void

Sometimes
I feel like a black hole
A cosmic void
That absorbs everything
Good and bad

My mind
Is in a turbulent uproar
Taking my body
Along for the ride

No matter how hard
I fight for dominion
Forces beyond my might
Keep me in a steel grip
Tyrannizing me
Till I'm at the cusp of madness

Then suddenly

They release me

Leaving me

Breathless

Weightless

Blissfully empty

Rainforest

It was a lone tree
Standing there

Breathing in and out

Waving its branches
Rustling its leaves

Breathing in and out

Sinking its roots deep
Into the fertile soil

Breathing in and out

Soaking up the sun
Drinking the groundwater

Breathing in and out

Cleansing the air

For all to inhale

Breathing in and out

Until the day they chopped it down

To make a new road

No more breathing in and out

Only an empty husk

A mere memory

No more breathing in and out

Putting us on the path

To destroy Mother Earth

No more breathing in and out

One tree after another chopped down

Our precious air stolen

Chain of Events

Waves breaking
Against my skull
Sending tremors
Down my spine
Ending in a stabbing pain
That radiates
Through my body
Turning my fingertips and toes
Completely numb
Scaring my heart
Into beating erratically
And my breaths
To come in short gasps
Suffocating panic
Clings to me
Enhancing everything
Until I'm a sobbing mess on the floor
Teeth chattering and body shaking
Unable to move an inch
Paralysed

Pandemic

It started slowly

Then picked up speed

Suddenly the death toll

Ripped through our minds

Creating chaos and panic

And the world stood still

Frozen in horror

Demanding answers

Demanding salvation

Fight

Damaged

Damaged
Barely holding on
Pushed to the limit
By unsweetened life

But
I am holding on
Drawing on my strength
From deep within

Joy
I'll fight for every smile
Every belly laugh
That heals my mind

Rage

I felt the rage!

A slithering snake

Winding its way

Around my neck

Choking the air

From my lungs

It spreads to my skin

A hot breath of anger

An unstoppable wildfire

Forcing its way

Towards my heart

Soon, it will be too late

I will say things

That can never be

Taken back

Or forgotten

Green-Eyed Beast Part One

Sometimes, I'm jealous
Following the lives of many
I watch them live
Every day
I see their accomplishments

And that's when it happens
The little green-eyed beast
Starts whispering in my ear

If you weren't sick...
You just need to try harder...
If, if, if....
And so, it goes

But I am sick
I can't just try harder

Green-Eyed Beast Part Two

Sometimes I'm jealous
I watch people get sick
Having to face death
And surviving

They recover
Almost to something better
They get to enjoy life
Which they deserve

And that's when it happens
The little green-eyed beast
Starts whispering in my ear

You're sick all the time...
You won't recover and become better...
Forever, ever, and ever...
And so, it goes.

I am sick
I can't just try harder

Green-Eyed Beast Part Three

Sometimes I'm jealous
I watch people find a partner
Fall in love and get married
Create a life and future

I see their lives
Watch their love unfold and blossom
They share their wonderful joy
With everyone around them

And that's when it happens
The little green-eyed beast
Starts whispering in my ear

No one deserves a sick partner...
You don't have anything to give...
Nothing at all...
And so, it goes.

I am sick
I can't just try harder

Green-Eyed Beast Part Four

Sometimes I'm jealous

I hate it!

But can't prevent it

I'm only human

I know it well by now

I can feel it sneak up

Perch on my shoulder

And prepare to whisper

And that's when it happens

The little green-eyed beast

Starts whispering in my ear

I'll always be here...

I'll never go away...

Never ever...

And so, it goes

I am sick

I can't just try harder

Green-Eyed Beast Part Five

Sometimes I'm jealous
The green-eyed beast
Whisper furiously in my ear
With but a thought

I banish him to the back of my mind
Knowing I can never be free of him
But I decide if I will listen

I am sick
But I will never let it bring me down!

Naked

I feel naked
In their eyes of them

They peel of layers
Until my soul is exposed

Vulnerable and desperate
Wanting to cover up and flee

Instead of freezing in place
Like a deer in the headlights

Waiting for their judgement
That is an inevitability

I stand up proud
I embrace my vulnerability

I am naked
But I am me

Tempus Fugit

Empty
Hollow
A shell of my previous self

Time glides by me
In a steady stream
I can't tell you what I did with it

It just disappears
Like the mist under the sun

Changes

Changes

Doubt

Fear

Slight excitement

Is this really necessary?

What is the point?

If not to grow

To unfold your wings

And show the world

That when it kicks you

You are able to get up

To adapt and carry on

However much it scares you

It's not in human soul to give up

To succumb to pity

Fight!

For you are worth it!

I

I do not need your advice

I need your support

I don't want health tips

I'm not like everyone else

I want a gentle hug now and then

I have tried everything

I don't need you to make it all harder

I want your compassion

I don’t want your pity

I am a fighter

I am not a victim

Battlefield

A flood of emotions
Tactile and tantalizing
One minute
Pain filled hatred
The next

Warring against each other
Inside my skull
Trying to break through
To evaporate into thin air
Leaving me

Hollow
Cold

Longing for the sweet pain
Of the battlefield
That now is empty

Poppies flourishing

Where blood was spilled

During the fight of the century

Their red colour

A reminder of desperate passion

Tearing two people apart

In a futile attempt

To hold onto love

Hunting

I'm a huntress of the night
Of the brilliant morning light
Chasing the seasons
For a bit to bite

I dream of the hunt
The proverbial chase
Deep under the covers
Where safety is the key

Ignorance

They break us down
As if we are condemned houses
Intent on rebuilding us in their image
Stealing our pride and individuality
Leaving pitiful drones in their wake

They do not care
That they break our spirits
As well as our bodies

How are we supposed to recover
When they keep tearing us down?

I Swore

I swore it would be done
And then forgotten

But it wasn’t forgotten
And the blame was mine

I seek forgiveness
Though it needed to be done

I beg of you
Free me of this mental anguish
You promised to absolve me

Wish

I wish I could

I wish I had the strength

I wish, I wish, I wish...

So many wishes

And so little hope

I'm not giving up

But sometimes

Exhaustion

Tears me apart

And then I have to

Settle for dreaming

Yet, I keep on wishing

Dignity

You will have to rip it off
My cold dead body
Before I give up
My dignity to you

I gave you everything
And yet you wanted
More than anyone deserved to demand

Some things in life
Are meant to be earned
To be proven worthy of
And you did neither

Your greed got the best of you
Loosing you the only thing
Making your life worth anything

I had hoped

You learned your lesson

But now you are back

Demanding more

As if it is your right

I have nothing left to give

But my dignity

And that

I will never part with

Bureaucracy Sucks!

Sometimes life just sucks
You work your ass off
Only to be a laughingstock
Or at least feel that way

Public services fuck with you
The bureaucracy drives you nuts
They chase you around
Making you feel like you are at fault

All that you end up with
Is stress and frustrations
Wondering where you went wrong
Leaving you exhausted

Ready to give up
To move on
And forget it all
But you persevere
And get things done

Beast

An explosion
A gut-wrenching explosion
Tearing at the heart

Such innocence
A cover for pure evil
Unleashed when least expected
With a devastating result

No consciences
No control
Pure animal instinct

Without the cover of darkness
Fooling all
Only to be bitten

And never ever forget again
The malicious intent
Branded forever on the soul

Arrrgghhh

I will kill you

Perforate your heart

And listen to your last breath

Rejoicing as your evil soul

Takes flight towards the underworld

Where Hel awaits

Ready to deliver the torments

That you so clearly deserve

Murder

There is murder in my heart

Disgusting and delightful

I reach for the feeling

Letting it fill my being

Coating my vision in red

As I scream towards the dark sky

A demon in disguise

Ready to tear and claw

Unleashing euphoria in my veins

Cruor

The gentle morning light
Is saturated in the stench of death

The stark imbalance between
The hope and desolation

Leaves me unsettled
Fractured beyond belief

Macabre delusions in pretty packages
Tempt me with oblivion

A heady gift that would end the torment
Yet disgrace who I really am

Dream

Mayhem

I am the darkness from where it once came
The footprints on my soul
A chilling reminder
Born ages ago
When the world was still new

I harbour no illusions
That mankind remembers me
Let alone pray to me

I now walk alone
In a new and strange world
Trying to define myself
To find my way
And claim my place

Mischief and mayhem
Awaiting to be unleashed

Void

The void regurgitates
A spectre of my anima
Covered in crimson roses

I rise from the vermillion stardust
Femme fatale of obscurity
A tale whispered during devastating storms

Cimmerian shade
Brings poisonous talons
Tearing flesh from the bone

The sweet coppery taste
Of fresh blood from the source
Calls forth my ravenous nature

Who braved my rebirth?
Brought me out
Of the primordial midnight?

Do they think themselves safe?
That I'm a docile female
Here to do their bidding?

My black heart sings with joy
As I unleash the carnage
Thousands of lifetimes in the making

I will raze the earth beneath my feet
Swallow their screams
and bathe in their pain

Poison

Teeth rip

Claws slash

Madness dances

A wicked jig

I bathe in blood

I revel in rage

Come

Come play with me

Meet your fate

Accept you Destiny

I am devil's snare

A sweet maddening poison

I thank you for your soul

I thank you for your sacrifice

Come

Come lay with me

I will show you the abyss

I will bring you to the edge

How sweet you taste

Your fear an aphrodisiac

Night retreats

Dawn approaches

Come

Come stay in the darkness

Your heart is in my hands

Your soul in tatters

The room is red

Your blood painting the walls

Nothing left

Nothing wasted

War

Darkness descends over the land

This land that used to be rich with greenery
Now burnt

My lonely heart can't fathom the change
And slowly pounds with hurt
The tears slide down my cheek
As I hear the distant cries of the people
That once dwelled here

The ghost of the dead
A stark reminder
Of the horrors
That have passed through here
The wounds of the earth
Still deep and bleeding
The crying still being heard

I am walking among the ashes
And scream at the powerless feeling
That comes over me

I was too late
The cry for help ravaged my soul

I slide the tip of my sword in the ground
With revenge in my heart
I will repay this

Looking high in the sky
Above me
The ravens swirl
With anticipation of a feast

And a feast they shall receive
As vengeance
Will be mine

Kitten

At times, she felt like a fraud
Telling herself lies
To get through the day
Ignoring the truth
To sleep at night

She didn't understand
How she could be so lost
When she had everything,
More than she ever wished for
Though apparently not all

She was going to sit
Dangling her feet off the bridge
Waiting for the tide to turn
And fill up the canal
So, she could end it all

All she could think of

Was the peace of mind

That awaited her

Below the surface

She heard a frail mewing

Getting up to look for it

All worries were forgotten

Only someone more desperate than her

Could make such a sound

The big eyes stared pleading

When she picked up

The furry little soul

Never had she felt such peace

As she did that moment

The frantic beat of the tiny heart

Brought tears to her eyes.

She stroked the kitten’s fur

Feeling like she could breathe

For the first time in her life

Red Poppy

I have wandered over battlefields
The ground saturated
In bloody memories
The screams of pain
A whisper in the wind

Phantom feelings
Of death's frigid breath
Fanning over my clammy skin
A desperate longing
For the end to come
Before I succumb to my nightmares
The very abyss that swallowed up
My fellow fighters

Oh, how I long
For the agonising pain to be gone
For the memories to vanish
From my tired psyche
And my mortal part
To release my aching spirit

Whether fought

In damp trenches o

Or scorching deserts

With simple bayonets

Or shredding machine guns

Precious lives are lost

Victims of distorted beliefs

Of zealots that have lost their humanity

The time of remembrance strikes again

Yet, we have not learnt anything

We still battle for superiority

For oil and other money-making schemes

Desecrating mother nature

And the descendants

That will inherit the land

Rain Dance

Clouds are gathering
A grey veil descends
Sensing the rain that is to come
Feeling the pressure
Crowding my body

A thin sheet of sweat
Covers my pale skin
The heat makes breathing hard
Yet the smell of honeysuckle
Sweetens the air

Soon, I will bathe
In the warm summer rain
Illuminated by lighting
Dancing to the beat of thunder
Surrounded by deities

The wind lifts my hair

Caressing my body

As I celebrate the life

Returning to the plants

Renewing the earth

Clean Slate

Dawn approaches
And the stars disappear

A new day breaks
With nothing to hold onto

Starting over yet again
White as snow

Blood, sweat, and tears
From the day before

Swallowed by darkness
Reborn in light

Acknowledgements

Thank you my darling Ira for pushing me when needed and always there to help when I get stuck. You are my rock and I appreciate you more than words can express.

I'm absolutely in love with my cover and I have Tash from Dazed Design to thank for that. Her artistic creations continually amaze and impress me. Her friendship is a huge bonus.

I also have to thank my publisher Butterdragons Publishing for making my dreams come true.

Last but not least. Thank you to my amazing readers. Keep fighting!

About Helle Gade

Helle Gade lives in Denmark with her little diva dog. She is a book blogger, poet, photographer, nocturnal creature, avid reader and chocolate addict. She has been writing poetry since 2011 and published four poetry collections since then. She has been fortunate to work with a bunch of brilliant authors and photographers on The Mind's Eye series. Her book Nocturnal Embers won the Best Poetry Collection with eFestival of Words.

Other BDP books by Helle Gade

Terrifying Love - A Halloween Anthology

Beautiful Tragedy - A Halloween Anthology

How To Tame A Wild Tempest

Dolce Amore

Poesi - A Collection of Poems Volume One